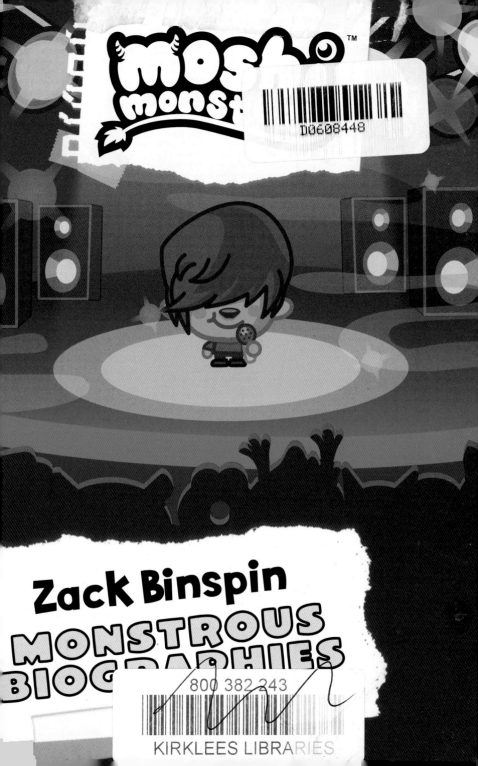

moshi
monst

Zack Binspin

MONSTROUS
BIOGRAPHIES

SUNBIRD
PENGUIN

Published by Ladybird Books Ltd 2013
A Penguin Company
Penguin Books Ltd, 80 Strand, London, WC2R 0RL, UK
Penguin Group (USA) Inc., 375 Hudson Street, New York 10014, USA
Penguin Books Australia Ltd, Camberwell Road, Camberwell,
Victoria 3124, Australia (A division of Pearson Australia Group Pty Ltd)
Penguin Group (NZ), 67 Apollo Drive, Rosedale, Auckland 0632,
New Zealand (a division of Pearson New Zealand Ltd)
Canada, India, South Africa

Sunbird is a trademark of Ladybird Books Ltd

Illustrations By Vincent Bechet
Written By Jonathan Green

www.ladybird.com

ISBN: 9781409391753
001
Printed in Slovakia

ALWAYS LEARNING

PEARSON

CONTENTS

Dedication

I dedicate this book to all my devoted fans out there.
You will always have a special place in my heart.

Love

ZACK

bbi SingSong

Foreword
By Simon Growl

Will this do, Ruby?

Yeah, er . . . thanks, Simon . . .

(I asked him to write a *foreword* for my book, not *four words*!)

Chapter 1

Teeny Moptop

Introduction

Zack Binspin is one of the hottest talents to be seen (and heard) on the Moshi Music scene in a long time. (He's certainly much cooler, more talented and way more handsome than another certain Moptop I could mention . . . but won't.)

Only recently signed to Moshi Music mogul Simon Growl's HighPants Productions hit factory, he's already worked with some of the best in the business. His partners in grime include the super-cool Flashy Fox rapper, DJ and all round diamond geezer Blingo. In fact, his break-through hit 'Moptop Tweenybop (My Hair's Too Long)' has made such a big impact on the music scene that Drool Metal legend Zommer has even recorded a rock-tastic cover of the track.

Zack was clearly always destined for gooperstardom, but the fame and fortune he's enjoying now is a far cry from his humble beginnings in Brashcan Alley — although he still keeps it real, hanging with his crew amidst the dustbins and piles of mouldering trash on the street.

As readers of the *Daily Growl* will already know, Zack Binspin is a close personal friend of mine (although you shouldn't believe everything you read in the press — unless it's in the pages of *Shrillboard Magazine*, of course). As a result I've been granted an Access All Areas backstage pass to find out everything any Moshi Music fan could possibly want to know about the biggest gooperstar in the world.

From Tiny Moshlings...

Sometimes it seems like some people have all the luck – being in just the right place at just the right time to be spotted by a major record producer, or being born into a background of wealth and privilege – but Zack Binspin's start in life didn't seem lucky at all.

Zack's parents were a goo collecting part-time mutant sprout tamer and a hairbrush saleswoman. Looking back now, it might seem like fate already knew what future it had in mind for Zack, but it wasn't so obvious to the young Tweenybop.

By three months he was already rubbing goo in his hair, as well as anything else he could get his hands on – including the lumpy gone-off mash his mum tried to feed him! By six months he was practising his dance moves and using one of his mum's hairbrushes as a pretend microphone.

The Streets of Monstro City

It was tough for the young Moshling growing up on the mean streets of Monstro City. And Brashcan Alley was about the toughest neighbourhood of the lot. It was here that the mutated results of some of Dr. Strangeglove's stranger experiments ended up after escaping from his sewer lair.

As every Moshi knows, that particular scientist is totally mad — well, so were the by-products of his monstrous meddlings. Bat-winged saveloy sausages*, freaky fanged fries, and burping burger baps, to name but a few. (Some say that Strangeglove was considering setting up his own fast food chain at the time!) Legend even has it that the mutant sprouts that roam Brashcan Alley were originally the result of another failed experiment involving mixing the ear wax of a Woolly Blue Hoodoo with a particularly potent growing potion.

Brashcan Alley was also the kind of place where grumpy Glumps went after being beaten again by the Super Moshis. It was a safe place to lick their wounds and come up with a good excuse before braving the wrath of Dr. Strangeglove. But this was the place Zack called home.

*Who said pigs can't fly?

The Magnificent Mutant Sprout Tamer

There weren't too many Rox to be made collecting goo or selling hairbrushes. To boost the family income in these hard times, from time to time Zack's dad would take his mutant sprout taming act on the road. And when he was old enough, the young Moptop Tweenybop would join him.

Zack idolised his father and watched every show with rapt attention from the front row – even though he had seen the act a hundred times before. It didn't take him long to catch the showbiz bug and develop the desire to perform himself.

Zack's dad would start the act with a joke or two to get the crowd warmed up, before getting down to the serious business of sprout-taming.

'What's the difference between sprouts and goo? Young Moshlings will eat goo! Unless they're mutant sprouts, of course, and then the answer's "Goo won't bite you back!" Ha-ha! Geddit? I tell you, it's the way I tell 'em...'

The sprout-taming show was the only entertainment the young Tweenybop was exposed to when he was small. The family were so poor they didn't even have Monstrovision!

Top of the Mops

While on the road with his dad, Zack would spend the long journeys trying out new hairstyles, using the goo his father collected to sculpt his luxurious locks. When he was old enough to be allowed out alone, he would walk the streets of Monstro City, and it was here that he discovered the wonders of Monstrovision. He would spend hour after hour standing outside the Moshi TV studios, watching whatever was showing on the TVs there. In fact, he watched so much TV it's amazing he didn't turn into a channel-hopping Monstrovision-obsessed Sneezing Panda!

His favourite programme was Top of the Mops. He would stand in front of the studio in all weathers, rain or shine, watching the bands performing on the show. But it wasn't until he saw a performance by Screech McPiehole that he realised his true calling.

Screech McPiehole is the legendary big-mouthed front man of those wrinkly monsters of rock, Hairosniff. He's been touring with the band for as long as anyone can remember, belting out classic hits to appreciative audiences all over Moshi world.

Seeing – and hearing! – Screech yelling along to his band on TV, at that moment Zack put two and two together and came up with a number one! The hairbrushes, the goo-tastic hairstyles, his pitch-perfect vocals . . . He would become a singer himself and one day sing on Top of the Mops, just like his idol Screech McPiehole!

Tucked up in bed that night, he dreamt of performing at the Hard Sock Café, the screams of his adoring fans making this teeny tiny Moshling feel as tall as the tallest totem pole in TikkiHaahaa.

But in spite of all his smooth moves and microphone mimicry, it didn't change the fact that Zack was just a Brashcan Alley brat. How was a Moptop like him ever going to be signed by some hotshot record producer?

It was then that Zack hit upon a clever idea. Loads of celebs seemed to spend much of their time hanging out at the Hard Sock Café and, if the ads in the Daily Growl were anything to go by, they were always looking for staff to wait tables there. Perhaps if he could get a job at the prestigious restaurant, he could get close enough to the movers and shakers in the Moshi Music biz to engineer the big break he was after.

Zack duly applied for the position of second assistant plate-scraper and was invited for an interview. But things didn't quite go according to plan from there on in.

The interview seemed to be going well until Zack said, 'An obvious example is Simon Growl. His are approximately two inches below his armpits.'

Puzzled, the interviewer asked, 'What on earth are you talking about?'

'You asked me to talk about high jean levels,' Zack replied.

He didn't get the job.

On his way home from the interview, feeling thoroughly dejected and despondent (and other words beginning with D), Zack turned into Brashcan Alley. Just when he was thinking his luck couldn't get much worse . . . he ran into a mob of Dr. Strangeglove's mischief-making Glumps!

Brashcan Alley Brawlers

Zack wasn't a tough Moshling, like Pocito the Mini Mangler. So as the mad doctor's minions bore down on him (no doubt planning on taking him away to be glumped), rather than fighting back like a Ninja would, he started singing instead.

The Glumps stopped, not quite believing what they were seeing – or hearing! And then Zack started to dance. He moonwalked like Blingo the Flashy Fox and strutted his funky stuff, just like Screech McPiehole on Top of the Mops. The Glumps were mesmerised! They just sat there, mouths open, staring at the Moptop Tweenybop as he danced and sang his way out of trouble.

Zack finished his performance with a flourish, and before the Glumps knew what was going on, he had scarpered back to his bin.

But Zack's parents had witnessed the whole thing from a distance, and had been impressed with the way their son kept a cool head in a crisis. They wanted something more for their pride and joy than to grow up and become a goo collector on Brashcan Alley. That evening, after another dinner of lumpy gone-off mash, they sat him down and his father asked him, 'What do you want to be when you grow up, my boy?'

Zack blushed. 'I want to be a singer, like Screech McPiehole.'

'You've got big dreams,' his mother said. 'You want fame.'

'Well fame costs,' his father went on, 'and right here's where you start paying. With goo!'

After that, Zack was set upon the path to gooperstardom, his parents backing him all the way – encouraging him to develop his singing voice, coaching him in hairbrush-microphone technique, and helping him perfect that flick of goo-styled hair.

But for Zack's dream to become a reality, Fate had to step in and give a helping hand.

Chapter 2
Search for a Gooperstar

The Next Big Thing

It wasn't only Zack's parents who had been impressed by the Moptop's singing.
As he faced off against the Glumps, another Tweenybop (and resident of
Brashcan Alley) had been chilling out in his bin, after a busy day in the
goodio. This toothy gooferstar had been tipped as the Next Big Thing, but
things weren't going well – there had been something lacking from the track
the Tweenybop had laid down that morning. Hearing Zack singing, the not-so-
superstar-in-the-making realised what it was at last!

It didn't take the dustbin diva long to track down the solution to his problems
and the very next day, Zack was singing backing vocals, bolstering the tooth-
some Moptop's own sadly lacking vocal talents. And that was how things stayed,
for a while.

Sometimes you can be inspired to do something better by seeing how badly
somebody else does it – and Zack's early experiences singing backing vocals for
the big-headed, bin-bound goofy wannabe-gooperstar are a perfect example.
You want proof? Nobody knows who that big-head is anymore, do they? The
only Moptop Tweenybop anyone remembers now is Zack Binspin! (Am I right, or
am I right?)

However, at the time the other Moptop was one of the biggest bin-bound
singers in Monstro City, but then Zack hadn't had his big break yet – just a
little one. Certainly, supporting another recording artist wasn't quite what Zack
had had in mind when he dreamt of singing on Top of the Mops, but it turned
out to be good experience in the end. And now that end was in sight.

18

Growl to the Rescue

When it comes to top Moshi Music producer and H.A.R.G.G. Simon Growl, there are four things that everyone agrees on:
1. He wears his trousers too high (like, right up to his armpits);
2. His hair looks ridiculous (but then it is a wriggly Wiggy Thing after all);
3. He's pretty clawsome at tracking down new musical talent;
4. He wears his trousers WAY too high.

   Like all of the recording stars topping the Moshi Music charts, Zack Binspin was discovered by the president and owner of HighPants Productions himself. But they didn't meet at some celebrity hang-out, like the Sandy Drain Hotel, and they didn't meet when Zack dropped by HighPants recording goodio with a demo he wanted to play the Growl-meister. They didn't even meet at the Underground Disco, where so many wannabes hope to achieve fame and fortune by showcasing their talents in front of the panel of celebrity judges. No, their meeting was way weirder than that – but clearly it was written in the stars... that Zack should become a star . . . or something . . .

A Funny Thing Happened on the Way to The Hard Sock Café

It all started when Simon Growl was hanging out in his luxury suite at the Sandy Drain Hotel on Music Island, ironing his extra high-waisted trousers. He had Moshi Radio on in the background as he was working on getting a really sharp crease down the front of his slim-line slacks, when suddenly the station's over-excited DJ announced that a toothy gooperstar would be performing a surprise gig at the Hard Sock Café, later the same day.

   It was certainly a surprise for the top talent scout and music producer. The gig must be secret if he didn't know about it! He decided, there and then, to fly back to Monstro City (via private jet) and check out the show for himself – after he had put his trousers back on, of course!

Zooming into Monstro City and landing at the airport, Simon made his way to the Hard Sock Café as quickly as he could by stretch limousine. As it turned out, the stretch limo was so long that when the driver pulled up outside the venue Simon was still at the other end of Main Street. He might as well have just walked to the gig!

His gooperstar credentials gave Simon an Access All Areas pass to any gig in Monstro City, so he took a seat in the front of the audience and waited for the show to begin.

Roary Scrawl, ace editor of the Daily Growl newspaper, has always got an eye (or ten) on what's going on in Moshi world. He was also at the Hard Sock Café, along with myself, taking photos and chatting with the gig-goers, ready to get the latest scoop on what was going down.

Now, I'm not a top music producer and talent scout myself, but to say that the show was a disaster would be an understatement. In fact, it was so bad, after only one song Simon Growl's Wiggy Thing gave a pained howl and scarpered – leaving poor Simon looking as bald as . . . well . . . Simon Growl without a Wiggy Thing on his bonce!

Suddenly as shy as a Bashful Bowlhead, Simon grabbed the nearest fuzzy thing there was to hand and stuck it on his head, to hide the fact that his hairpiece had done a runner (perhaps he didn't fancy being papped without his legendary hairdo in place) and took off after the wayward Wiggy Thing.

He did look ridiculous with a Tubby Huggishi plonked on his head – pink really isn't Simon's colour! – but at least he had managed to avoid having his nude noggin photographed and plastered across the front page of the Daily Growl when the newspaper hit the newsstands the following morning.

Lost!

Stumbling out of the venue, with the Huggishi clinging to the top of his head and its fluffy fur in his face, the top music producer couldn't actually see where he was going.

Pushing aside the curtain of pink fur from before his eyes, Simon Growl gave a gasp of surprise when he saw where he had ended up. In Brashcan Alley!

He was totally freaked out, totally lost and not knowing what else to do, took out Gabby his Mini Moshifone to call for help. It was then that he heard the sound of someone singing echoing tinnily down Brashcan Alley. This was nothing like the singing of the goofy-toothed wannabe that had scared his Wiggy Thing away at the secret gig. It wasn't great – it was absolutely fan-trash-tic!

At that moment Simon Growl knew that he had discovered the newest, ultimate singing sensation. Now all he had to do was find out who they were and where they were hiding! But as it turned out this was going to be easier sung than done!

23

Chapter 3
New Lid on the Block

Singing in the Drain

So there was Simon Growl, loitering in Brashcan Alley with a Tubby Huggishi plonked on top of his head, wondering which dustbin the sensational singing had come from.

The trouble with Brashcan Alley is that it's teeming with Tweenybops, the grotty garbage that litters the street creating the perfect habitat for these manky Moptops. Whole families live in dumpsters, while others – like Zack's dad – spend much of their time collecting goo from the mash-choked gutters. So how was Simon supposed to tell which battered bin was the battered Binspin bin?

Two things made this task even harder for him. First of all, he didn't know it was the Binspin bin he was looking for, and secondly the Huggishi's tail was still flapping around in front of his face. As Simon put it when I interviewed him for this book, 'We are all in the gutter, but some of us are looking for the stars.'

Straining to hear through all the Huggishi's fur, Simon focused all of his pop-tastic powers on his surroundings, trying to block out any background noise. And sure enough, his talent-radar didn't let him down. Approaching the bin, he knocked on the lid, wondering who could possibly be making that angelic warbling sound.

There was no answer.

Simon Growl isn't the kind of Moshi who likes to be kept waiting. That, coupled with the fact that he still felt uncomfortable being stuck in Brashcan Alley, meant that he reacted a little more impatiently than he might have done otherwise. Receiving no reply to his knocking, Simon gave the bin a kick instead.

Now normally this wouldn't have mattered, except that on this occasion Simon had forgotten he was wearing the 'look taller' platform boots he had bought at the Marketplace, to make an even bigger entrance – or at least a taller one – when he turned up at the surprise gig earlier that evening unannounced.

One whack from the kind of ridiculously high-heeled footwear you'd expect to see being worn by a gooey glam rock rocker like Sweet Tooth was enough to send the dustbin flying into a putrescent pile of gross-out garbage. Simon simply stood there, his pink kitty wig stand-in still sitting on his head, his mouth agape, a gasp of shock frozen on his face.

The lid of the bin rolled away along the gutter. Accompanied by a few heartfelt moans and groans, Simon's superstar-to-be crawled out of the trash can, covered in bogus bacon rind and stinky six day-old leftover scrambled eggs.

Garbage in, Garbage out

As the Moshling wiped the foul food from his face, Simon laid eyes on Zack Binspin for the first time, and saw that the Moptop Tweenybop was wearing headphones! That explained why he hadn't heard Simon knocking.

The gooperstar producer (and winner of the Highest Waistband in Pop award three years in a row) was so relieved that Zack was all right that he came to a startling sudden decision. Realising that X marked the spot in this grimy back alley, he was ready to offer the mucky Moptop a multi-million rox recording contract right then and there. But as he opened his mouth to speak, an ominous beeping sound began to echo from the walls of Brashcan Alley.

Before Simon could even say, 'Hi, I'm Simon Growl, music producer, owner of HighPants Productions and all round HAARG,' a huge garbage truck had reversed into the alleyway and scooped up the entire pile of trash – Zack Binspin included!

Simon Growl's newest disco discovery was heading for the Monstro City dump, and it was all the music producer's fault! It looked like Zack's music career was going to be over before it had even begun!

Chapter 4
A Gooperstar is Born

Call Me Gabby

It was crunch time! At least something was going to go crunch if Simon didn't do something to save Zack in time! But Simon couldn't do anything until he had got the snoozing Huggishi off his head (and his Wiggy Thing back in place) and was looking his best. After all, he didn't want to be caught out in another potentially embarrassing prowling paparazzi incident, did he?

It was then, as he was wondering how he was going to save Zack from the garbage crusher – or worse still a life of bin-bound obscurity! – that Simon had a brilliant idea. Taking out Gabby, his Mini Moshifone, he asked the tiny Techie to summon his wayward Wiggy Thing using her high-pitched whistling ringtone.

Sure enough, after a few toots – which also scared off that lazy Huggishi – Simon Growl was reunited with his furry friend, and he could finally see where he was going again. Only he didn't set off after the garbage truck for the Monstro City dump, but back to his mega massive mansion instead!

You see, just like they don't do their own laundry or clean their own private pools, gazillionaires like Simon Growl don't hang out in stinky landfill sites. Oh goodness no! Mega-rich stars like Simon Growl hire other monsters to do that sort of thing for them.

Meanwhile, at Growl Mansion . . .

Once he was home, Simon sent his driver, Bubba the Bouncer's brother, to fetch Zack from the dump. Needless to say, Zack was pretty shaken up when he arrived at Growl Mansion, although Simon seemed to think that it was down to the humble Tweenybop meeting him for the first time, rather than because of Zack's hair-raising experience at the city dump.

Without even giving the poor Moptop a chance to recover his breath or calm his n-n-n-nerves, he immediately laid out his plans for the Moptop's Moshi Music career – telling him he had a chance of appearing on the producer's splat-tastic new Music Rox album – and signed his dump-dazed new discovery on the spot!

Simon hurried Zack into the goodio at once, knowing that he had the perfect track for the Moptop to record, and with which to launch his chart-busting career. You see the song had originally been earmarked for another well-known Moptop but it turned out that he wasn't actually any good – in fact he was utterly ghastly! – so Simon decided to see what Zack could do with it instead. The Moptop made the song his own in no time.

And so a gooperstar was born.

Anatomy of a Gooperstar

Now Simon Growl's no singer (whatever he might try to tell you himself) but he is the ultimate pop Svengali, the leader of the pack, the guy who's gang you want to be in if you want to make it big in the Moshi Music biz! If it wasn't for the HighPants producer's vanity, the world might have been denied the wonder that is Zack Binspin. Just imagine it – a world without Zack's pitch-perfect vocals and goo-tastic hair! It doesn't bear thinking about!

One of the pop-tastic talents that Simon possesses is knowing what makes the perfect popstar and recognizing those talents in others. And of course Zack Binspin had everything a hit supremo could ever hope to find in any up-and-coming talent.

So what is it that makes one Moptop just another Tweenybop and then a Moptop like Zack Binspin a chart-busting trash-tastic phenomenon? Is it really just all down to natural charm, good looks, and a mega-hit factory writing and producing team? Or is there something fundamentally different about their make-up at a genetic level?

I, Ruby Scribblez, have carried out my own exhaustive research to find out what it is about Zack Binspin that makes him so fangtastically incredible. Well, what I actually mean is I borrowed one of Dr. Strangeglove's chemistry sets and a hair from Zack's head, but things didn't quite work out as I had planned. (I hope that Titchy-Tusked Mammoth forgives me for turning its hair green!)

Having failed when it came to the appliance of science, I gave up on the whole genetic analysis thing and went for dinner with Simon and Zack instead and just asked them. Here's what they told me.

A Big Heart
If you want to make it big in the music biz, you're going to need a big heart – one that's full of love for all your adoring fans (and yourself). If you love the fans, they'll love you back. And the more love a smouldering gooperstar's fans have for their Moptop idol the higher the star's star will rise!

Frog in the Throat
The bane of singers everywhere! Lose your voice and it could be curtains for your Moshi Music career. So, whatever you do, look after your voice – and lay off the Toda Sodas!

Flutterbies in the Stomach
They say it's good to feel a little bit nervous before going on stage; that way you give your best performance. So a few Flutterbies in the stomach is a good thing, and certainly not a reason to reach for the Wobble-ade!

Funny Bone
A good sense of humour helps if you're going to survive in the Moshi Music biz. If you can laugh off the tough gigs and bad reviews then you might just manage to keep yourself together, and avoid ending up like that well-known sugary psycho Sweet Tooth!

Extra Thick Skin

You might be the biggest Moshi Music megastar in the Moshi World, but there's always going to be someone who will try to take you down a peg or two. You're going to need a skin as thick as a Snoring Hickopotumus's to be able to put up with their put-downs.

Gooey Good Looks

Cute as Kissy the Baby Ghost, gooey good looks go a long way towards transforming a mere Moshling into a musical megastar.

Hip Happening Hair

It takes hours of grooming with a fishbone comb and plenty of goo to get a Moshling's Moptop looking this good. But it's worth all the effort. After all, the bigger the hair, the bigger the star!

Jukebox Voicebox

A true gooperstar has the vocal range to sing anything from a low Z to a high Q! The greater your range, the greater your chances of scoring a Number One hit.

Hip Hipsta Hip Action

Smooth moves and cool dance steps are always going to wow the crowds, but if you're going to be able to pull them off, you've got to remember that it's all in the hips.

Paw-tapping Toes

If you're going to be writing, singing and generally performing paw-tapping tunes, you need to be able to tap your paws in time to your own tremendously paw-tapping paw-tappers.

Chapter 5
Chart Throb

Goo've Got the Look

It cannot have escaped your notice that Zack Binspin is the coolest, cutest, trash-tastically charming, crooning Moshling Moptop there is, but it takes time and effort – and lots of practice – to be this naturally talented and good looking.

'So how does Zack maintain his goo-licious good looks?' I hear you cry.

Well, you just answered that question yourself

Goo!

Zack never goes anywhere without his fishbone comb and plenty of gooey hair gel. It's essential for him to give his moptop that shiny, just-stepped-out-of-a-pile-of-garbage look that his fans go weak at the knees for.

But although Zack had the look that Simon Growl was searching for, there was still some way to go before the impressive impresario could happily sit back and say that he had managed to mould the Moptop into the perfect popstar. In fact, talking of going weak at the knees, to make sure that Zack didn't do precisely that when he was performing on stage, he enlisted the help of Blingo the Flashy Fox.

Now Blingo is better known as a super slick DJ and funky fly rapper – you know, the one that every rising rocker wants to work with. Known for his rap-tastic lyrics that he delivers in his strange, lightning fast language, he's so cool Wistful Snowtots are boiling hot by comparison! Oh, and of course he never takes off his shades because if he did he would be totally dazzled by all that gleaming bling he wears!

But what's less well-known is that Blingo is also a cunning choreographer. Check out his signature moonwalk if you're not convinced.

The Bling's the Thing

The Flashy Fox was set the task of devising the ultimate dance routine to accompany Zack's debut single – one that his adoring fans could pick up easily – and to make sure that the Moptop practised his cool dance moves, sometimes for up to ten minutes, every day! Without fail! Ten minutes! Just imagine it. Now that's real dedication!

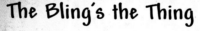

As well as getting Blingo to sort out Zack's dance steps, Simon also got him to lay down one of his funkadelic raps on what he hoped would be, the Moptop's breakthrough solo single. It was a dream come true for Zack to get to work with the funky fly rapper. After all, all the chart-topping Moshi Musicians want the Flashy Fox to lay down some radical rhymes over their latest Monster-tastic track.

When I was backstage at one of Zack's gigs, hanging out with him in his dressing room before he went on stage, I asked him to take me through his shimmyin' and shakin' dance routine – the one that accompanies the chorus of 'Moptop Tweenybop (My Hair's Too Long)' – one step at a time.

1. First stamp with your left foot.

2. Now stamp with your right foot.

3. Swing those hips left and right.

4. Now do it again, twice, at double speed.

5. Shuffle left, but holding your right arm out from your side.

6. And now shuffle right, with your left arm out.

7. Pump your hands over your chest like a beating heart.

8. Moonwalk on the spot while pulling your arms backwards and forwards.

9. Put your hands to your face and shake those hipsta hips again.

10. Drop to your knees with your arms out wide from your body.

Radio Blah-Blah

So Zack had the look sorted, a goopendous debut track laid down, and a dance routine worked out. It was time for Highpants Productions publicity machine to go into overdrive, making sure that his name was soon on everyone's lips.

As part of the promotion process, Zack appeared on Moshi Radio... I mean, I say appeared, but you can't see anything on the radio, so obviously what I really mean is that Zack was interviewed in the Moshi Radio goodio . . . for the show Music Island Discs.

When he was asked to name the top ten tunes he would want to have downloaded on his Eye-Pod if he was stranded on a desert island for an afternoon – tunes, not Tunies; that would just be ridiculous – this is the list of records Zack chose.

Zack Binspin's Top Ten Tunes

1. Moptop Tweenybop (My Hair's Too Long) - Zack Binspin
2. Moptop Tweenybop (My Hair's Too Long) - Zack Binspin
3. Moptop Tweenybop (My Hair's Too Long) - Zack Binspin
4. Moptop Tweenybop (My Hair's Too Long) - Zack Binspin
5. Moptop Tweenybop (My Hair's Too Long) - Zack Binspin
6. Moptop Tweenybop (My Hair's Too Long) - Zack Binspin
7. Moptop Tweenybop (My Hair's Too Long) - Zack Binspin
8. Moptop Tweenybop (My Hair's Too Long) - Zack Binspin
9. Moptop Tweenybop (My Hair's Too Long) - The Zommer Remix
10. Diggin' Ya Lingo - Blingo

When asked why he would take so many copies of his own song to his desert island, Zack replied, 'In case something happened to one of them I want to make sure I've got a spare or two.'

Binspin-Mania

Of course, being a roarsome gooperstar does come with its drawbacks. As his fame grew, so did his fan base. Soon, Moshlings all over Moshi world were wanting to meet their Moptop idol, and some of them seemed prepared to do just about anything to achieve their goal.

Everywhere Zack goes he finds himself mobbed by Moshling music-lovers that the monster press have dubbed Tweenyboppers. And some of these Tweenyboppers can be very inventive when it comes to trying to find ways to get into Zack's presence.

Take the (not so) Bashful Bowlhead, for example, who managed to get into Zack's hotel room once, disguised as part of his room service order! Or the Lipsmacking Bubbly who tried the very same thing the next day. Or the Sweet Ringy Thingy who tried the exact, self-same trick the day after that . . .

In the end, to keep his megastar safe from over-enthusiastic fans, Simon Growl had to employ Bubba's brother to be Zack's personal bodyguard. Bubba's brother has even been known to pick up Zack's bin and carry him to gigs – sometimes even hitching a ride on the back of a garbage truck – to make sure the gooperstar gets there at all!

Zack's fans have displayed such high levels of love and devotion that a term has been coined to describe the phenomenon – Binspin-Mania!

Even though some of their attempts to get close to him give Zack's management cause for concern, Zack's fans mean the world to him. If it wasn't for them and their support, he wouldn't be the gooperstar he is today.

To pay them back for their love and devotion, Zack asked me to set up an official fan club for all the Moptop Tweenyboppers and Zack Pack Wannabes out there. I, Ruby Scribblez, was its first official member of course – but then I am Zack's number one fan! Every month I prepare a newsletter for the fan club, listing anything Zack's devoted followers could possibly want to know about the megastar, from where his next personal appearance is going to be, to what he has on his rider at every gig.

If you've ever considered joining yourself, here's a few pages from the latest issue of the newsletter.

How to Draw Zack Binspin

Are you one of Zack's biggest fans? Have you ever thought how cool it would be to be able to draw your own picture of the Moptop Tweenybop megastar? Well now you can - in three easy steps!

Step 1
Draw a circle for his head.

Step 2
Draw a rectangle for his body.

Step 3
Draw the rest of Zack Binspin.

MOSHI
TOP

Zack's 'Binpsin Tour' Rider

Many Rox megastars are almost as famous for their epic riders as they are for their music. (In case you don't know, a rider is a set of requests that a performer makes before even agreeing to do a gig. Talk about high maintenance!) Some are notorious while others are just down right silly.

But what about Moshi World's newest superstar singing sensation? What is it that Zack's manager Simon Growl says has to be backstage at every one of the Moptop Tweenybop's gigs? Well, I'll tell you . . .

Posters of his idol Screech McPiehole decorating the walls of his dressing room

A large mirror - I'll give you one guess

Plates of lumpy gone-off mash and some mutant sprouts - in case he gets peckish

GOOEY
HAIR GEL

A fishbone comb - for styling his hair

Gooey hair gel - also for styling

His 'Best Moptop's Moptop' award - voted for by the readers of Shrillboard Magazine (and its editor!)

A battered trash can with a rusty bin lid - for when he just wants to kick back and relax or grab a few Zs after a gig

BEST
MOPTOP

A Roarshall amp - so that everyone at the gig can actually hear his super-sweet, super-soft, pitch-perfect singing

Roars'

His personal security guard Bubba's brother, on guard at the stage door

EXIT

A gaggle of adoring fans ready to scream 'We love you, Binspin!' at the stage door

Ruby Scribblez Gooperstar Giggles

Q: What do you call someone who hangs around with musicians?
A: A drummer.

Q: What is the difference between a guitar and a tuna fish?
A: You can tune a guitar, but you can't tuna fish.

Q: How many lead singers does it take to change a light bulb?
A: One. He holds the bulb while the world revolves around him.

Chapter 6
Livin' the Dream

Fame and Fortune

Zack's fame and fortune have of course led to him being able to enjoy opportunities and experiences that the son of a goo collector and hairbrush saleswoman could never have expected to come his way.

When Zack thinks back to his early childhood, growing up in Brashcan Alley – just a few months ago! – watching Screech McPiehole on Top of the Mops, and wishing that one day he could do the same, he realises that these days he really is living the dream! He gets to hang out at the coolest clubs – he's permanently on the guest list at the Underground Disco – he gets to perform at the swankiest venues – such as the Hard Sock Café – and he can now count among his friends, gazillionaire music producers and blinged-up rapper foxes.

When he's not on tour, laying down new tracks in the goodio, or being interviewed and snapped by the paps, Zack likes nothing better than chillaxing with his new celebrity friends at the Sandy Drain Hotel.

There's plenty for your typical, totally un-average, celeb to do at Music Island's hippest hang-out, from enjoying a range of gooey spa treatments or tucking into a monster-rific meal at the gourmet restaurant, to taking a dip in the hotel's world famous guitar-shaped pool or paddling in the surf on the Sandy Drain's private beach. Such luxury is all on tap if you can afford it – but then it is only mega-rich megastars who can afford to stay at the highly exclusive hang-out in the first place.

What's even better is that all of these activities can be indulged in away from the prying eyes of Moshlings like Shelly the Nattering Nutling and her snap-happy pal Holga.

A Day in the Life of a Gooperstar

So what is a day in the life of the Moshi World's biggest musical discovery since the Sugardrum Mountains on Music Island like?

Seeing as how I'm a close personal friend of the star, I snuck a look at Zack's personal diary when we were hanging out the other day in his blinged up bin on Brashcan Alley – all in the name of investigative journalism, of course!

So here's what a typical day in the life of the one and only Zack Binspin is like!

9.00am Woke up and went to the bathroom. Checked my hair. This was an early start – if I had been at a gig last night I would have demanded to lie in until around midday

9.10am Having checked my hair, went back to bed.

10.00am Got up again. Checked my hair. Went to grab a glass of Essence of Blue, but I was right out, so glugged a Slug Slurp Slushie instead. Put on my headphones, so I could listen to some classic Hairosniff, and then went back to bed again.

11.00am Simon Growl gave me a call on his Mini Moshifone but I missed it, 'cos I had my headphones on.

11.10am Having rung a couple more times, Simon sent Bubba's brother round to give my bin a kick. Realising that someone was trying to get my attention, I got up and opened the lid.

11.15am Went to the bathroom again. Checked my hair and began my morning styling routine. Combed my hair, added some goo, tried out a new style,

added some more goo, combed my hair again, added just a little more goo, tried a different style... bit more goo, bit more combing . . . went back to my usual style (which my fans all love) and as soon as I couldn't see myself in the mirror through all my hair (it's too long, you know) I knew I was ready for the day.

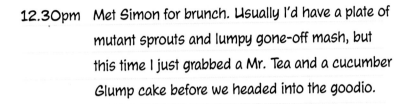

12.30pm   Met Simon for brunch. Usually I'd have a plate of mutant sprouts and lumpy gone-off mash, but this time I just grabbed a Mr. Tea and a cucumber Glump cake before we headed into the goodio.

1.00pm   Having laid down some totally trash-tastic tracks (featuring my to-die-for pitch-perfect vocals) we headed over to Music Island on Simon's private jet and hung out with some of our other megastar muso friends by the pool at the Sandy Drain Hotel.

4.00pm
Flew back to Monstro City, ready for that night's gig, and was greeted by adoring, screaming fans at the airport. Having taken some time to sign a few autographs I headed into town for a public appearance

HIGH PANTS

and another signing session before taking part in another Moshi Radio interview.

5.00pm Dinner at Hard Sock Cafe. Made a change from just running my hands through my hair and snacking on whatever I found in there.

6.00pm Headed to the gig venue, where a whole team of stylists, choreographers and musicians were

waiting to help me get ready. I don't know why Simon bothers, I do my own hair, I've got the moves like Blingo, and I've got pitch-perfect vocals to die for. There's nothing for the team to do!

7.00pm Gig time!

7.01pm On the way from my dressing room to the stage I just stopped to check my hair one last time. Comb – check! Goo – check! Eye-obscuring fringe – check! I was good to go!

7.10pm The gig started – a little late – but my fans don't mind.

8.00pm After shimmyin' and shakin', and setting the Poppets' pulses racing, the gig was over and I left the stage, and my fans screaming for more.

8.02pm I went back on stage for one last encore of 'Moptop Tweenybop (My Hair's Too Long)'. When that was done, I left the stage again (and my fans screaming for more – again).

8.12pm On the way from the stage door to Simon's waiting limo I signed some more autographs,

had my photo taken with a bunch of adoring Moshlings, and generally basked in the love of my loyal fans. Then it was off to the after party at the Underground Disco to chillax with my friends. Simon took a turn spinning the wheels of steel while I wowed the gang with more of my shimmyin' and shakin'. And then we partied into the early hours.

The Early hours – I headed back to Brashcan Alley and crashed in my crusty crib ready to do it all again tomorrow.

A Lot of Good Work for Chari-dee

Zack hasn't forgotten his humble roots and as a way of saying thank you for everything that fame and fortune have brought him, he does a lot of good work for charity.

Most of his fund-raising efforts go to help Hairpeace, which works hard to unite those who are folically-challenged with abandoned Wiggy Things – giving one a home and the other hair again!

The President of Hairpeace is Simon Growl and their motto is, of course, hair today, gone tomorrow.

HAIRPEACE

★ Hair today, gone tomorrow ★

Chapter 7
Just a Brashcan Alley Brat

There's No Place Like Home

Since signing to his high-trousered mentor's record label, Zack would argue that the life of a fabulously wealthy singer-songwriter-gooperstar hasn't changed him at all – he's still just as cute, conceited and pitch-perfect as he was the day when Simon Growl stumbled across his bin in Brashcan Alley!

When he's not hanging out with his new pals at the Sandy Drain Hotel, this particular Moptop Tweenybop likes to keep it real by getting back to his funky dustbin down on the street where he grew up. It's here he really feels at home, surrounded by mutant sprouts, lumpy gone-off mash, and piles of stinking trash. Although of course he's had his bin redecorated since making it big.

Zack's Blinged-Up Brashcan Alley Crib

1. Siren Party Plinth
P – A – R – T – Y? Cos he's gotta! There's no stopping the party prince from getting down and having a good time with his friends. And when the siren sounds you know that tonight's gonna be a good night!

2. Furry Luv Chair
From every monster's favourite furniture shop – and furniture don't get much Yukea than this one!

3. Framed Gold Disc
Zack received this for selling... ooh, probably loads and loads of copies of 'Moptop Tweenybop (My Hair's Too Long)'. It's bound to be only the first, with many more to come.

4. Disco Glitterball & Crash Mat Dance Floor
Zack lives for music and he never knows when the need to show off some of his smoothest moves might hit him, so he's got his own sprung dance floor (so he doesn't hurt himself when he's break dancing) and a disco glitterball ready to go, just in case.

5. Decent Decks
It's not unheard of for that Flashy Fox Blingo to drop by Zack's Brashcan Alley pad, and when he does he likes nothing better than spinning a few discs, while the Moptop Tweenybop tries copying Blingo's signature moonwalk move.

6. Cutest Moshling of the Week Award
This was awarded to Zack by the Pretty Poppets Cute Club. (I actually got to present him with that one myself!)

7. Framed Shrillboard magazine front cover
When Zack hit the big time, Shrillboard Magazine was not slow in declaring him the 'poster boy for Moptop Tweenyboppers everywhere', featuring him on the front cover.

8. Davy Gravy's Guitar
Signed by the lead singer of the Goo Fighters, it's just for show. Zack might be the greatest singer in Moshi world, but he can't play a musical instrument for toffee (or for Sludge Fudge, for that matter).

9. Bling Wallpaper
Zack is so rich now that he can afford to cover the walls of his trash can with Rox!

Hanging with Bobbi SingSong

When Zack needs somewhere to get away from it all, he heads over to Jollywood to spend some quality time with fellow RoxStar, Bobbi SingSong, at his secret yoga retreat. Ommmm!

59

Binspin on Tour

When taking his music on tour around Moshi world, Zack stays in an enormous tour bus or a super-luxury hotel. Here's some exclusive snaps from his most recent tour!

Hangin' on the tour bus

Crowdsurfin'

Oops!

Party Time

Moptop Tweenybop

Zack's career is only just beginning, but he's already the biggest gooperstar in Moshi World. I for one can't wait to see where his music – or his hair – takes him next.

So for now, this is where our story ends. And since it's always good to end on a high note, take it away Zack!

MOPTOP TWEENYBOP (My Hair's Too Long)

Hey... you wanna stroke my hair? It's okay... it's just me, Zack, Zack Binspin
Hey, check out my lid. It's real rusty.
Conditioner? No, this is just goo baby.

I live in a funky dustbin
Surrounded by trash
We're talking 'bout mutant sprouts
And lumpy, gone-off mash

Yeah, I gotta funny hairdo
But hey that's okay
If you run your fingers through it, it's like a buffet

Moptop Tweenybop
Shimmyin' an shakin'
I've lost count of the hearts that I've been breakin'
I can't see and my eyeballs they are achin',
cos my hair's too long

I hang out in Brashcan Alley
With my band and my crew
If you were a true believer, you'd be there too

Yeah I know that I'm a heart throb
But that ain't a crime
So check out my dustbin, baby
We can snuggle in the grime

Moptop Tweenybop
Shimmyin' and shakin'
I've lost count of the hearts that I've been breakin'
I can't see and my eyeballs they are achin',
cos my hair's too long

I'm here with my homies in the crazy world of Moshi
Rappin' for my buddy even though he's wishy washy
Slamming down the rhymes like a rusty dustbin lid
Blingo the Fox?! Duetting with a kid?
Moptop Tweenybop shimmyin' and shakin'
Sittin' on his groove, you know that I ain't fakin'
Holy guacamole I just gotta rap more slowly
Cos I'm runnin' outta breath and these tempo's kinda throw me

Moptop Tweenybop
Shimmyin' an shakin'
I've lost count of the hearts that I've been breakin'
I can't see and my eyeballs they are achin',
cos my hair's too long

We love you Binspin
I know!

The End